Inside My World

MY DAY AT SCHOOL

By Tina Benajmin

Gareth Stevens
PUBLISHING

Please visit our website, www.garethstevens.com. For a free color catalog of all our high-quality books, call toll free 1-800-542-2595 or fax 1-877-542-2596.

Library of Congress Cataloging-in-Publication Data

Benjamin, Tina.
My day at school / by Tina Benjamin.
p. cm. — (Inside my world)
Includes index.
ISBN 978-1-4824-1802-6 (pbk.)
ISBN 978-1-4824-1800-2 (6-pack)
ISBN 978-1-4824-1801-9 (library binding)
1. Schools — Juvenile literature. 2. School day — Juvenile literature. I. Benjamin, Tina. II. Title.
LB1513.B45 2015
372—d23

First Edition

Published in 2015 by
Gareth Stevens Publishing
111 East 14th Street, Suite 349
New York, NY 10003

Editor: Ryan Nagelhout
Designer: Sarah Liddell

Photo credits: Cover, p. 1 Brocreative/Shutterstock.com; p. 5 littleny/Shutterstock.com; pp. 7, 9, 21 Hurst Photo/Shutterstock.com; pp. 11, 24 (desk) sdecoret/Shutterstock.com; pp. 13, 15, 17 Monkey Business Images/Shutterstock.com; pp. 19, 24 (basketball) Robert Kneschke/Shutterstock.com; p. 23 rSnapshotPhotos/Shutterstock.com.

Printed in the United States of America

CPSIA compliance information: Batch #CW15GS: For further information contact Gareth Stevens, New York, New York at 1-800-542-2595.

Contents

Today is Monday.
I am going
to school today!

I have a blue backpack.
I carry my books in it.

I ride on a school bus.
I sit with my friend Liza.

We go to class.
I have my own desk!

A B C D E F G H I J K L M
a b c d e f g h i j k l m
0 1 2 3 4 5 6 7 8 9 10 11 12 13 14 15 16 17 18 19 20 21 22 23 24 25 26 27 28

I like my teacher.

She teaches us
about animals.

I go to lunch.
I love to eat lunch
with my friends.

I go to gym.
We play basketball!

I take the bus
home, too.

HOOL DIST.

The bus driver drops me off at my house.
My school day is over!

SCHOOL BUS
EMERGENCY DOOR
SLOW

Words to Know

basketball

desk

Index

SCHOOL BUS
SLOW

Words to Know

basketball

desk

Index